Planning for Learning through CLOTHES

Rachel Sparks Linfield and Christine Warwick

Illustrated by Cathy Hughes

Contents

Published by Step Forward Publishing Limited

The Coach House, Cross Road, Milverton, Leamington Spa, CV32 5PB Tel: 01926 420046

© Step Forward Publishing Limited 2000

Planning for Learning through Clothes   ISBN: 1-902438-31-0

MAKING PLANS

WHY PLAN?

The purpose of planning is to make sure that all children enjoy a broad and balanced curriculum. All planning should be useful. Plans are working documents that you spend time preparing, but which should later repay your efforts. Try to be concise. This will help you in finding information quickly when you need it.

LONG-TERM PLANS

Preparing a long-term plan, which maps out the curriculum during a year or even two, will help you to ensure that you are providing a variety of activities and are meeting statutory requirements of the Early Learning Goals.

Your long-term plan need not be detailed. Divide the time period over which you are planning into fairly equal sections, such as half terms. Choose a topic for each section. Young children benefit from making links between the new ideas they encounter so, as you select each topic, think about the time of year in which you plan to do it. A topic about minibeasts will not be very successful in November!

Although each topic will address all the learning areas, some could focus on a specific area. For example, a topic on clothes would lend itself well to activities relating to Personal, Social and Emotional Development and Creative Development. Another topic might particularly encourage the appreciation of stories. Try to make sure that you provide a variety of topics in your long-term plans.

Autumn 1	People who help us
Autumn 2	Autumn/Christmas
Spring 1	Nursery rhymes
Spring 2	Clothes
Summer 1	Toys
Summer 2	Minibeasts

MEDIUM-TERM PLANS

Medium-term plans will outline the contents of a topic in a little more detail. One way to start this process is by brainstorming on a large piece of paper. Work with your team writing down all the activities you can think of which are relevant to the topic. As you do this, it may become clear that some activities go well together. Think about dividing them into themes. The topic of Clothes, for example, has themes such as 'Socks and shoes', 'Clothes for all weathers', 'Uniforms' and 'Clothes from around the world'.

At this stage, it is helpful to make a chart. Write the theme ideas down the side of the chart and put a different area of learning at the top of each column. Now you can insert your brainstormed ideas and will quickly see where there are gaps. As you complete the chart, take account of children's earlier experiences and provide opportunities for them to progress.

Refer back to the Early Learning Goals document and check that you have addressed as many different aspects of it as you can. Once all your medium-term plans are complete, make sure that there are no neglected areas.

DAY-TO-DAY PLANS

The plans you make for each day will outline aspects such as:

- resources needed;
- the way in which you might introduce activities;
- the organisation of adult help;
- size of the group;
- timing.

Identify the learning that each activity is intended to

MAKING PLANS

promote. Make a note of any assessments or observations that you are likely to carry out. On your plans, make notes of which activities were particularly successful, or any changes you would make another time.

A FINAL NOTE

Planning should be seen as flexible. Not all groups meet every day, and not all children attend every day. Any part of the plan can be used independently, stretched over a longer period or condensed to meet the needs of any group. You will almost certainly adapt the activities as children respond to them in different ways and bring their own ideas, interests and enthusiasms. The important thing is to ensure that the children are provided with a varied and enjoyable curriculum that meets their individual developing needs.

USING THE BOOK

* Collect or prepare suggested resources as listed on page 21.

* Read the section that outlines links to the Early Learning Goals document (pages 4 - 7) and explains the rationale for the topic of Clothes.

* For each weekly theme, two activities are described in detail as examples to help you in

your planning and preparation. Key vocabulary, questions and learning opportunities are identified.

* The skills chart on page 23 will help you to see at a glance which aspects of children's development are being addressed as a focus each week.

* As children take part in the Clothes topic activities, their learning will progress. 'Collecting evidence' on page 22 explains how you might monitor children's achievements.

* Find out on page 20 how the topic can be brought together in a grand finale involving parents, children and friends.

* There is additional material to support the working partnership of families and children in the form of a 'Home links' page, and a photocopiable 'Parent's page' found at the back of the book.

It is important to appreciate that the ideas presented in this book will only be a part of your planning. Many activities that will be taking place as routine in your group may not be mentioned. For example, it is assumed that sand, dough, water, puzzles, floor toys and large scale apparatus are part of the ongoing pre-school experience, as are the opportunities which increasing numbers of groups are able to offer for children to develop ICT skills. Role-play areas, stories, rhymes and singing, and group discussion times are similarly assumed to be happening in each week although they may not be a focus for described activities.

USING THE EARLY LEARNING GOALS

Having decided on your topic and made your medium-term plans, you can use the Early Learning Goals to highlight the key learning opportunities your activities will address. The goals are split into six areas: Personal, Social and Emotional Development; Communication, Language and Literacy; Mathematical Development; Knowledge and Understanding of the World; Physical Development and Creative Development. Do not expect each of your topics to cover every goal but your long-term plans should allow for all of them to be addressed by the time a child enters Year 1.

The following section highlights parts of the Early Learning Goals document in point form to show what children are expected to be able to do by the time they enter Year 1 in each area of learning. These points will be used throughout this book to show how activities for a topic on Clothes link to these expectations. For example, Personal, Social and Emotional Development point 7 is 'form good relationships with peers and adults'. Activities suggested which provide the opportunity for children to do this will have the reference PS7. This will enable you to see which parts of the Early Learning Goals are covered in a given week and plan for areas to be revisited and developed.

In addition, you can ensure that activities offer variety in the goals to be encountered. Often a similar activity may be carried out to achieve different learning objectives. For example, when children make hats from circles in Week 6, they will be learning about shape but they will also be exploring aspects of technology as they fold the paper, cut and glue. It is important, therefore, that activities have clearly defined goals so that these may be emphasised during the activity and for recording purposes.

PERSONAL, SOCIAL AND EMOTIONAL DEVELOPMENT (PS)

This area of learning covers important aspects of development that affect the way children learn, behave and relate to others.

By the end of the Foundation Stage, most children will:

PS1 continue to be interested, excited and motivated to learn

PS2 be confident to try activities, initiate ideas and speak in a familiar group

PS3 maintain attention, concentrate and sit quietly when appropriate

PS4 have a developing awareness of their own needs, views and feelings and be sensitive to the needs, views and feelings of others

PS5 have a developing respect for their own cultures and beliefs and those of other people

PS6 respond to significant experiences, showing a range of feelings when appropriate

PS7 form good relationships with adults and peers

PS8 work as a part of a group or class, taking turns and sharing fairly, understanding that there need to be agreed values and codes of behaviour for groups of people, including adults and children, to work together harmoniously

PS9 understand what is right, what is wrong and why

PS10 dress and undress independently and manage their own personal hygiene

PS11 select and use activities and resources independently

PS12 consider the consequences of their words and actions for themselves and others

PS13 understand that people have different needs, views, cultures and beliefs, that need to be treated with respect

PS14 understand that they can expect others to treat their needs, views, cultures and beliefs with respect

The topic of Clothes offers many opportunities for children's personal and social development. Time spent discussing favourite clothes, how to look after clothes and reasons for wearing uniforms will encourage children to speak in a group, to be interested and to consider consequences. By playing circle games, children will learn to take turns and to understand the need for agreed codes of behaviour. Many of the areas outlined above, though, will be covered on an almost incidental basis as children carry out the activities described in this book for the other areas of children's learning. During undirected free choice times, they will be developing PS11 whilst any small group activity that involves working with an adult will help children to work towards PS7.

COMMUNICATION, LANGUAGE AND LITERACY (L)

The objectives set out in the *National Literacy Strategy: Framework for Teaching* for the reception year are in line with these goals. By the end of the Foundation Stage, most children will be able to:

L1   enjoy listening to and using spoken and written language, and readily turn to it in their play and learning

L2   explore and experiment with sounds, words and texts

L3   listen with enjoyment, and respond to stories, songs and other music, rhymes and poems and make up their own stories, songs, rhymes and poems

L4   use language to imagine and recreate roles and experiences

L5   use talk to organise, sequence and clarify thinking, ideas, feelings and events

L6   sustain attentive listening, responding to what they have heard by relevant comments, questions or actions

L7   interact with others, negotiating plans and activities and taking turns in conversation

L8   extend their vocabulary, exploring the meaning and sounds of new words

L9   retell narratives in the correct sequence, drawing on language patterns of stories

L10   speak clearly and audibly with confidence and control and show awareness of the listener, for example by their use of conventions such as greetings, 'please' and 'thank you'

L11   hear and say initial and final sounds in words and short vowel sounds within words

L12   link sounds to letters, naming and sounding letters of the alphabet

L13   read a range of familiar and common words, and simple sentences independently

L14   show an understanding of the elements of stories such as main character, sequence of events, and openings and how information can be found in non-fiction texts to answer questions about where, who, why and how

L15   know that print carries meaning and, in English, is read from left to right and top to bottom

L16   attempt writing for different purposes, using features of different forms such as lists, stories and instructions

L17   write their own names, and other things such as labels and captions, and begin to form simple sentences, sometimes using punctuation

L18   use their phonic knowledge to write simple regular words and make phonetically plausible attempts at more complex words

L19   use a pencil and hold it effectively to form recognisable letters, most of which are correctly formed

The activities suggested for the theme of Clothes include several that are based on well-known, quality picture books and stories. They allow children to enjoy listening to the books and to respond in a variety of ways to what they hear, reinforcing and

extending their vocabularies. Throughout the topic, opportunities are described in which children are encouraged to use descriptive vocabulary and to see some of their ideas recorded in both pictures and words. A variety of role-play areas, such as a shoe shop and a ticket office for the fashion show, are used to encourage children to enjoy listening to and using written and spoken language in their play.

MATHEMATICAL DEVELOPMENT (M)

The key objectives in the *National Numeracy Strategy: Framework for Teaching* for the reception year are in line with these goals. By the end of the Foundation Stage, most children will be able to:

M1 say and use number names in order in familiar contexts

M2 count reliably up to ten everyday objects

M3 recognise numerals 1 to 9

M4 use language such as 'more' or 'less' to compare two numbers or quantities

M5 in practical activities and discussion begin to use the vocabulary involved in adding and subtracting

M6 find one more or one less than a number from one to ten.

M7 begin to relate addition to combining two

groups of objects and subtraction to 'taking away'

M8 talk about, recognise and recreate simple patterns

M9 use language such as 'circle' or 'bigger' to describe the shape and size of solids and flat shapes

M10 use everyday words to describe position

M11 use developing mathematical ideas and methods to solve practical problems

M12 use language such as 'greater', 'smaller', 'heavier' or 'lighter' to compare quantities

The theme of Clothes provides a meaningful context for mathematical activities. Children are given the opportunity to count shoes, toes, socks, gloves and national costume dolls and to begin to develop language for addition and subtraction. Shoes are used as non-standard units for measuring. There are opportunities for children to explore shape, pattern and size as they compare soles of shoes and make card people, native American Indian head-dresses, bonnets and paper clothes.

KNOWLEDGE AND UNDERSTANDING OF THE WORLD (K)

By the end of the Foundation Stage most children will be able to:

K1 investigate objects and materials by using all of their senses as appropriate

K2 find out about, and identify, some features of living things, objects and events they observe

K3 look closely at similarities, differences, patterns and change

K4 ask questions about why things happen and how things work

K5 build and construct with a wide range of objects, selecting appropriate resources and adapting their work where necessary

K6 select the tools and techniques they need to shape, assemble and join materials they are using

K7 find out about and identify the uses of everyday technology and use information and communication technology and programmable toys to support their learning

K8 find out about past and present events in their own lives, and in those of their families and other people they know

K9 observe, find out about and identify features in the place they live and the natural world

K10 begin to know about their own cultures and beliefs and those of other people

K11 find out about their environment and talk about those features they like and dislike

The topic of Clothes offers many opportunities for children to make observations, to ask questions and to compare. They can explore the differences and similarities in shoe prints and observe the way chocolate melts as they make marshmallow top hats. As children investigate waterproof materials and the best way to wash clothes, they will gain a greater understanding of the properties of materials. Through talking to people who wear uniforms and looking closely at the clothes, children will be able to find out about and identify features of uniforms.

PHYSICAL DEVELOPMENT (PD)

By the end of the Foundation Stage, most children will be able to:

PD1 move with confidence, imagination and in safety

PD2 move with control and coordination

PD3 show awareness of space, of themselves and of others

PD4 recognise the importance of keeping healthy and those things which contribute to this

PD5 recognise the changes that happen to their bodies when they are active

PD6 use a range of small and large equipment

PD7 travel around, under, over and through balancing and climbing equipment

PD8 handle tools, objects, construction and malleable materials safely and with increasing control

The fashion show provides a useful stimulus for encouraging children to move with control and co-ordination. A variety of activities such as pretending to dress for a long, cold walk or getting dressed in a morning will give children the opportunity to move with imagination. Balancing equipment is used as children pretend to go outside, dressed for a range of weather conditions.

CREATIVE DEVELOPMENT (C)

By the end of the Foundation Stage most children will be able to:

C1 explore colour, texture, shape, form and space in two or three dimensions

C2 recognise and explore how sounds can be changed, sing simple songs from memory, recognise repeated sounds and sound patterns and match movements to music

C3 respond in a variety of ways to what they see, hear, smell, touch and feel

C4 use their imagination in art and design, music, dance, imaginative and role play and stories

C5 express and communicate their ideas, thoughts and feelings by using a widening range of materials, suitable tools, imaginative and role play, movement, designing and making, and a variety of songs and musical instruments

During this topic, children will experience working with a variety of materials as they make collages of people, sock puppets, hats, necklaces and bonnets. They will be able to develop their skills of painting and colour mixing as they paint themselves wearing their favourite clothes and so work towards C1 and 4. A number of songs that have actions fit into the clothing theme and have been suggested to allow children to use their imaginations in music. Throughout all the activities, children are encouraged to talk about what they see and feel as they communicate their ideas in painting, collage work and role play.

Week 1

MY CLOTHES

PERSONAL, SOCIAL AND EMOTIONAL DEVELOPMENT
- During a circle time, show the group some of your favourite clothes. Talk about why they are special. Encourage children to talk about their own favourite clothes. (PS2, 3)

- Show the group some clothes which have been taken off and are inside out. Demonstrate how to turn clothes the right way out and how to fold shorts, trousers, a T-shirt and a jumper. Invite children to have turns at folding clothes and encourage them to tidy their own clothes away after times such as PE and painting. (PS4, 8, 10)

- Set up the home corner with a basket of laundry, plastic coat hangers, a suitcase, a toy ironing board and iron. Encourage the children to take part in role play, washing clothes, tidying them and packing a case ready for a holiday. (PS8, 11)

COMMUNICATION, LANGUAGE AND LITERACY
- Read *Mrs Lather's Laundry* by Allan Ahlberg (Puffin). Later in the week, show children the days of the week written on strips of card. Use the days of the week signs and the pictures in the book to help children retell the story of Mrs Lather in their own words. (L3, 9)

- Read the story of Paddington Bear's arrival in London found in *Paddington's Story Book Treasury* by Michael Bond (Harper Collins). Paddington arrives in England with just one suitcase. Ask the children to imagine that they are going on a long journey. What clothes would they take in their bag? Make small card suitcases (see activity opposite). (L3, 19)

- Begin a washing basket word bank. Cut items of clothing from large pieces of card and write the name on each. Use the clothing to play 'I spy' games and for sorting the clothing according to initial sounds. (L11, 13)

MATHEMATICAL DEVELOPMENT
- Use *Jerry's Trousers* by Nigel Boswall and David Melling (Macmillan) as the stimulus for counting activities (see activity opposite). (M2, 3)

- Provide each child with a jumper and a hat cut from A4 white paper. Use circular and square sponges and ready-mixed paints to cover them with matching, repeating patterns. (M8, 9)

- Provide each child with clothes cut from card. Encourage the children to place the clothes on a drawn washing line in a repeating pattern. Help the children to be aware of sizes, colours and types of clothing. (M8)

KNOWLEDGE AND UNDERSTANDING OF THE WORLD
- Compare babies' and children's clothes. Talk about the sizes and the styles and how much children grow from when they are babies. (K1, 3)

- Investigate the best way to wash pieces of fabric stained with paint. (K1)

- Invite a parent to talk to the group about how they wash clothes for their children. Look at pictures of how washing used to be done. Talk about the changes that have taken place. (K8)

- Investigate different ways in which clothes can be fastened. Sort clothes according to whether they have Velcro, buttons, zips or studs. Talk about the reasons for the different types of fastenings. (K1, 4)

PHYSICAL DEVELOPMENT
- Tell a story of waking, getting up and choosing clothes to wear outside. Encourage children to mime convincingly with imagination. (PD2)

- Play 'Simon says' in which the actions are all associated with clothes. (PD1)

- Sing and put actions to the song 'Here we go round the mulberry bush'. Encourage children to skip during the chorus. Sing the song slowly and quickly to allow the children to skip at varying speeds in time with the tune. Use the verses of 'This is the way we .... ' for miming putting on and wearing a wide range of clothes. (PD1)

CREATIVE DEVELOPMENT
- Help children to paint pictures of themselves wearing their favourite clothes. (C1)

- Use scraps of material, brightly coloured paper and pieces of ribbon to decorate people cut out from card in clothes children would like to wear. (C1, 5)

- Provide each child with a square cut from A4 sized paper. Ask children to fill their square with clothes cut from mail order catalogues and magazines. Once filled, use the squares to make a giant clothes patchwork. (C1)

ACTIVITY: Packing a suitcase

Learning opportunity: Writing name labels for suitcases, listening to and responding to a story.

Early Learning Goal: Communication, Language and Literacy. Children will be able to listen with enjoyment and respond to stories. They will use a pencil and hold it effectively to form recognisable letters, most of which are correctly formed.

Resources: *Paddington's Story Book Treasury* by Michael Bond (Harper Collins) or a similar version; suitcases made from folded A4 card; luggage labels.

Key vocabulary: Suitcase, pack, names of clothing.

Organisation: Whole group.

WHAT TO DO:

Read or tell the story of Paddington Bear's arrival in London. Look at pictures of Paddington and his suitcase. Ask children why they think he came to London and what he would have needed on his journey. Then ask children what they would like to have in a suitcase if they were going on a long journey. Talk about the kinds of clothes they would need, food and also things to keep themselves busy on the journey.

Provide each child with a piece of A4 sized card folded in half and two handles cut from card. Show them how to stick the handles onto their cases and ask them to draw inside all they would pack. Some children may also like to write the words of the things in the cases or the initial sounds. Finally, help children to write or trace over their names on a luggage label and attach these to the suitcases.

ACTIVITY: Number clothes line

Learning opportunity: Learning to recognise and to order the numbers from one to nine.

Early Learning Goal: Mathematical Development. Children will be able to count reliably up to ten everyday objects and will recognise numerals 1 to 9.

Resources: *Jerry's Trousers* by Nigel Boswall and David Melling (Macmillan); washing line; clothes pegs; nine pairs of trousers cut from card with the numbers 1 to 9 written on them.

Key vocabulary: Numbers one to nine, clothes line.

Organisation: Whole group.

WHAT TO DO:

Read *Jerry's Trousers* by Nigel Boswall and David Melling (Macmillan). Talk with children about all the trousers which Jerry wore and the variety of patterns on them. Show children the clothes line and explain that you have nine pairs of trousers to hang on the line. Ask children to help you check that you do have nine. Show the group a pair with the number 5 written on them. Ask if anyone knows what it says. Peg it in the centre of the line. Show children the other pairs and look at the numbers. Explain that you would like the clothes to be arranged in number order and invite children to peg them on the line. Ask the children to shut their eyes. Remove a number and ask which trousers have disappeared.

DISPLAY

Cut out the children's portraits and place them with the collage people on a frieze of a street scene. Invite children to choose the place where they would like their people to go. Mount the magazine clothing squares on black sugar paper to give a 2cm border. Display the squares together to make a large patchwork. Around the patchwork place questions to encourage children and parents to look for different clothes and to count similar ones.

Week 2
SOCKS AND SHOES

PERSONAL, SOCIAL AND EMOTIONAL DEVELOPMENT

- Make a collection of different types of shoes including ones that are good for walking, sports, parties, sandals, boots and slippers. Encourage children to think about when the shoes might be worn and why. (PS2, 9)

- Demonstrate how to polish shoes. Afterwards, as a group, sequence the stages of shoe polishing. (PS1, 3)

- Talk about the importance of taking good care of shoes and the need to keep them tidy in pairs. Decorate clothes pegs for keeping wellington boots in pairs (see activity opposite). (PS12)

COMMUNICATION, LANGUAGE AND LITERACY

- Begin a word bank of words which rhyme with feet, shoe and toe. Help children to write the words on shoes cut from card and to decorate the shoes. (L18, 19)

- Enjoy sharing stories in which shoes feature, such as the traditional fairy tales of 'The Elves and the Shoemaker' and 'Cinderella'. (L3)

- Read 'Socks' by John Coldwell in *What's In a Number?* (Walker Books). Discuss the variety of socks in the poem. Which of the socks would the children enjoy wearing? Give each child a sock cut out from paper to decorate as if it was one of the socks described in the poem. (L1, 3)

- Read and enjoy *Six Feet Long and Three Feet Wide* by Jeannie Billington and Nicola Smee (Walker Books). Discuss how feet were used to measure the size of beds and why the beds were different sizes. (L3)

MATHEMATICAL DEVELOPMENT

- Help children to draw around one of their own feet, cut it out and use it as a non-standard measure of length. (M2, 9, 12)

- Draw around both feet of each child, including each toe. Ask children to cut out the feet and arrange them in pairs. Encourage the children to count the number of toes on each foot and in each pair. (M2)

- Use cut-outs of children's feet for sorting according to size. Show children a foot and ask them to select feet which are longer than/shorter than/the same size as it. (M9, 12)

- Sort socks into pairs. Count the number of socks and the number of pairs. (M1, 2)

KNOWLEDGE AND UNDERSTANDING OF THE WORLD

- Make a collection of clean shoes and sort them into groups according to their fastenings. Ask the children which shoes are easiest to fasten. Can anyone tie up laces? Enjoy learning how to tie bows. (K1, 2)

- Make a collection of old shoes and trainers which can be used for printing using paint. Investigate patterns on the soles. Talk about the importance

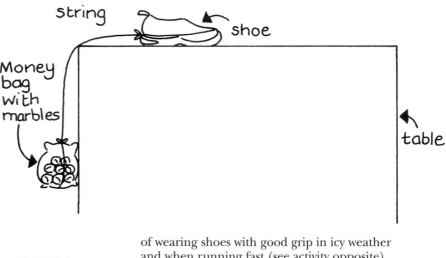

of wearing shoes with good grip in icy weather and when running fast (see activity opposite). (K1, 3)

- Use a trainer and a smooth soled shoe of the same size to investigate which would be best to wear to prevent slipping. Place one of the shoes on a table, attach a plastic coin bag to the shoe and see how many marbles are needed to make the shoe move (see diagram). (K1, 2, 4)

PHYSICAL DEVELOPMENT

- Help children investigate the many ways they can use their feet to move. Encourage them to enjoy hopping, skipping, striding, jumping, and so on. (PD2)

- Practise moving along balancing equipment.

Encourage children to move steadily, feeling the equipment with their feet. (PD2)

- Challenge the children to walk or hop with a bean bag balanced on one of their feet. (PD2)

CREATIVE DEVELOPMENT

- Help children to make puppets out of socks. Enjoy using them in collaborative role play. (C1, 4)

- Use clean, worn-out tights to make snakes. Give each child one leg cut from a pair of tights. Fill the leg with scrunched-up tissue paper and knot the end. Decorate the snake with a variety of brightly coloured scraps of paper, fabric and sequins. (C1)

- Use shoes to make sounds. Show how feet can tip-toe quietly, stamp loudly and skip quickly. Play a game in which children use their feet to tap out nursery rhymes. Can the group guess which rhyme is being played? (C2)

- Set out the role-play area as a shoe shop. Include a cash register, telephone, receipt book, pairs of shoes in boxes labelled with sizes and an instrument for measuring foot size. (C4)

ACTIVITY: Printing with shoes

Learning opportunity: Observing soles of shoes and looking for similarities and differences.

Early Learning Goal: Knowledge and Understanding of the World. Children will be able to investigate objects by using all of their senses as appropriate and look closely at similarities, differences and patterns.

Resources: Ready-mixed or thick powder paint; sponges larger than the shoe soles; trays for the paints; black sugar paper.

Key vocabulary: Names for the shoes, sole, names of the paint colours, print, press.

Organisation: Small group.

WHAT TO DO:

As a group, look at the soles of the shoes and describe the patterns. Which shoes do the children think will help people not to slip? Why? Explain to the group that they are going to make prints of the shoe soles. Prepare a sponge for printing by covering it in paint and placing it in a tray. Show the children how to place a hand inside a shoe and press it onto the painted sponge before pressing it in the centre of their black sugar paper. Demonstrate how to hold the shoe firmly and steadily to avoid a smudged print.

Look at the patterns. Are they what the children expected them to be like? When all children have finished printing, wash the shoes and cut out the prints. Match the prints to the shoe soles.

ACTIVITY: Making boot pegs

Learning opportunity: Talking about the need to take care of possessions and considering ways to keep boots tidy.

Early Learning Goal: Personal, Social and Emotional Development. Children will be able to consider the consequences of their words and actions for themselves and others.

Resources: A bag of shoes and boots; for each child a wooden clothes peg named with a permanent pen; piece of card; crayons; scissors and glue.

Key vocabulary: Lost, tidy, pair, shoe, boot.

Organisation: Whole group.

WHAT TO DO:

Show the group the bag of boots and shoes. Explain that you have a friend who is untidy. She finds it difficult to find her boots and shoes when she has to go out. Ask the group to suggest things that could help your friend to be tidier. Can they help you sort the footwear into pairs?

Talk about the importance of taking care of belongings. Show the group a peg and suggest that each child could take one to decorate and name for keeping their own boots or shoes in a pair. Demonstrate how to draw a person, animal, flower, boat, car or house on a piece of card; colour it and cut it out; then stick it on the clothes peg. Encourage children over the following weeks to use their pegs for keeping their shoes tidy whenever they are taken off.

DISPLAY

Arrange the snakes on a background of large leaves cut from a variety of shades of green sugar paper. On a nearby table put out the sock puppets placed over plastic bottles weighted with sand. Peg the decorated paper socks on a string washing line. Above the line write out the sock poem. Cut out the shoe prints and display these on a board. Place the real shoes close by to encourage children to look closely at their patterns and to match the sizes. This display is particularly effective if the shoe prints are laminated.

Week 3

CLOTHES FOR ALL WEATHERS

PERSONAL, SOCIAL AND EMOTIONAL DEVELOPMENT

- Look at pictures of people dressed for a variety of weathers. Discuss the different clothes that people are wearing. What would children choose to wear if it was cold? Why? What do people wear when it is raining? (PS2)

- Put out a box of dressing-up clothes for a range of weathers. Encourage children to enjoy trying on the clothes and to talk about the occasions when they might wear their chosen outfits. (PS2, 10)

- Play the weather clothes miming game in which children take it in turns to mime putting on an item of clothing for friends to guess what it is. Encourage children to mime to show how the clothing is fastened and worn, and to think of the weather for which the clothing would be suitable. (PS8)

COMMUNICATION, LANGUAGE AND LITERACY

- Make catalogues of clothes for all weathers (see activity opposite). (L16, 17)

- Read *Tattybogle* by Sandra Horn and Ken Brown (Hodder Children's Books). Discuss the way that the wind spoiled the scarecrow's clothes. Ask children to think about the clothes they would like to wear if they were scarecrows who had to be outside in all weathers. (L3)

- Introduce the group to 'Dress the Teddy' on *My World* computer program (see Resources page). Talk about the clothes Teddy might need for different weather conditions and encourage the children to dress Teddy in a variety of clothes using the program. (L7)

MATHEMATICAL DEVELOPMENT

- Provide children with a sheet of pictures of gloves and mittens in a variety of sizes and patterns. Help the children to colour match those which are the same. Count how many gloves there are and how many pairs they make. (M2, 8)

- Play a beetle drive type game in which children shake a die and collect clothes to dress a doll. (M1, 3)

- Provide each child with a paper scarf with nine sections in which the numbers one to nine are printed. Encourage the children to match counters to each number on the scarf. (M2, 3)

KNOWLEDGE AND UNDERSTANDING OF THE WORLD

- Investigate which materials are waterproof (see activity opposite). (K1, 3)

- Make a collection of old pairs of wellington boots. Use the boots to make wet footprints outside. Encourage children to describe the prints, to match prints with the boot soles and to notice how the wet prints disappear as the water evaporates. (K1, 3, 4)

- Make a collection of a wide range of materials. Encourage the children to look closely at each material, to describe its texture and to select scraps which would be suitable for wearing on a cold/rainy/hot day. Give each child a person cut from card and ask them to stick their selected materials on it to make a person dressed for particular weather. (K1, 2)

PHYSICAL DEVELOPMENT

- Encourage children to imagine that they are going on a long walk and make up a story including events and activities which will need a change of clothes on the way. First they need to dress. Then they must fill a large rucksack with changes of clothing to suit a variety of weather. Help children to think about the types of clothes they might pack and to move imaginatively according to the descriptions given in the story. (PD1, 3)

- Tell children a story of dressing warmly to go outside on a windy day. The wind is very strong and children need to walk slowly, feeling their way so as not to be blown away. Encourage children to walk carefully as they use a range of balancing equipment as bridges, and so on. (PD6, 7)

- Enjoy having dressing-up races using clothes for all weathers. (PD3)

CREATIVE DEVELOPMENT

- Provide each child with a drawing of a body with a line drawn vertically down the middle. Ask children to draw and colour clothes to dress half

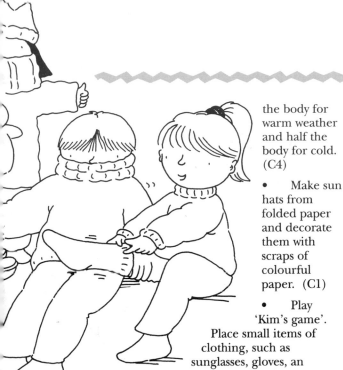

the body for warm weather and half the body for cold. (C4)

• Make sun hats from folded paper and decorate them with scraps of colourful paper. (C1)

• Play 'Kim's game'. Place small items of clothing, such as sunglasses, gloves, an umbrella, swimming costume, and so on, on a tray. Encourage children to look closely at the objects, touch and describe them. Cover the tray with a cloth and ask children to recall as many items as they can. (C3)

ACTIVITY: All-weather clothing catalogue

Learning opportunity: Writing names and making catalogues.

Early Learning Goal: Communication, Language and Literacy. Children will be able to attempt writing for different purposes and will write their own names.

Resources: For each child a piece of A4 sized card folded in half with 'Clothes for all weathers chosen by .... ' written on the front and the words 'sun', 'rain' and 'snow' on the remaining pages; clothing catalogues; magazines; pencils; scissors; crayons; glue.

Key vocabulary: Sun, rain, snow, weather, names for chosen items of clothing.

Organisation: Small group.

WHAT TO DO:

Show children a clothing catalogue and help them to understand how catalogues are set out with similar types of clothes in sections. Explain that they are going to make their own catalogues for different weathers. Show them the cards prepared for the catalogues. Help them to distinguish between the pages for rain, snow and sun. Talk about the different clothes which might appear on each page. Provide each child with a clothing catalogue and invite them to cut out their favourite clothes for the three weathers and to stick them in their own catalogues. Finally, help the children to write or trace their own names on the front of the catalogues. Some children may also wish to label the clothes in their catalogues.

ACTIVITY: Investigating materials

Learning opportunity: Predicting, observing, describing and comparing.

Early Learning Goal: Knowledge and Understanding of the World. Children will be able to investigate materials by using all of their senses as appropriate and they will look closely at similarities and differences.

Resources: 30 cm squares cut from plastic, towelling, cotton and net; a picture of people dressed for rainy weather.

Key vocabulary: Waterproof, soak, plastic, cotton, net, towelling, wet.

Organisation: Small group.

WHAT TO DO:

Show children the picture of people dressed in waterproof clothing. Talk about the types of clothes that the people are wearing and ask why they would be useful. What do children wear when it is raining? Why? Pass the squares of material around the group. What do they feel like? Would any of them be good outside on a rainy day?

Explain to the group that they are going to help to find a material for making a raincoat for a teddy bear. The material must not soak up water or let it pass through. A good raincoat is one where the water runs off. Fasten each square over a plastic beaker with an elastic band. Invite children in turn to stand the beaker in a plastic tray, pour a tablespoon of water over the material and to describe what happens. Afterwards compare the amounts of water which have passed through the materials and the dampness of each material. As a group decide which material would be best for a raincoat.

DISPLAY

Make a background, on a large noticeboard, of a range of weather conditions including rain, sun, snow and wind. Invite children to position their collage people in the most suitable place for the clothing worn. On a table set out clothing items for children to play 'Kim's game' and nearby arrange the pictures of people wearing clothes for hot and cold weather.

Week 4

UNIFORMS

PERSONAL, SOCIAL AND EMOTIONAL DEVELOPMENT

- During a circle time, brainstorm the variety of uniforms of which children are aware. Talk about the reasons for wearing uniforms. (PS1, 3)

- Invite a Brownie, Guide, Beaver or Cub to show their uniform and to talk about what it means to belong to their group. (PS1, 3)

- Encourage children to make and send thank-you cards to all the visitors who come in during the week to show their uniforms (see Knowledge and Understanding of the World). (P3, 4, 7)

COMMUNICATION, LANGUAGE AND LITERACY

- Read *Mrs Jollipop* by Dick King-Smith (Macdonald Young Books). Look at the pictures of Mrs Jollipop's uniform and discuss why it would be a good uniform for a lollipop lady. Look closely at Mrs Jollipop's 'Stop' sign. Help children to find other words which rhyme with 'stop' and to write them on signs. (L3, 17)

- As a group, make a dictionary of uniforms. Invite children to draw pictures of people wearing uniforms. Discuss how the uniforms could be sorted. For example, ones which are the same colour might go on the same page. Encourage children to write or trace over their own names to label their pictures. (L17, 19)

- Enjoy reciting 'The Grand Old Duke of York' from *Pudding and Pie* chosen by Sarah Williams (Oxford University Press). Discuss what children think the duke might have looked like and whether his men wore a uniform. (L3, 4)

MATHEMATICAL DEVELOPMENT

- Use pictures of football players for sorting activities. Sort by colour and by pattern. Encourage children to count how many players are in each set and to compare the numbers. (M2, 4)

- Play the football clothing game (see activity opposite) (M2, 4)

- Use coloured sticky shapes to decorate football shirts made from stiff paper. Encourage children to name the shapes they used. (M9)

KNOWLEDGE AND UNDERSTANDING OF THE WORLD

- Help children to investigate which colours can be seen easily. Look at pictures of uniforms and consider which ones really stand out. Encourage children to think of reasons for the colours of a range of uniforms. (K1, 3)

- Invite an adult, known to the group, who wears a uniform for work to come and show the uniform. Ask them to explain why their uniform is useful. Ask children to design a new uniform for the adult. (K2)

- Show children pictures of uniforms, such as the one worn by Brownies which have changed over the years. Look at and describe similarities and differences. Why do the children think the changes have taken place? Which uniforms do the children prefer? (K3)

PHYSICAL DEVELOPMENT

- Help children to practise walking gracefully in a straight line, turn smoothly and stand still, ready for the fashion show. (PD2)

- Provide each child with a coloured band to wear to play games in teams. Talk about the usefulness of the bands as a uniform for identifying the different teams. (PD2)

- Give each child a bean bag and show them how to balance the bean bags on their heads. How far can each child walk without losing the bean bag? (PD2)

CREATIVE DEVELOPMENT

- Provide a range of uniforms in the dressing-up area to encourage imaginative role play. (C4, 5)

- Make jointed people to dress in uniforms for a display of a football game (see activity below). (C1)

- Enjoy singing songs about people who wear uniforms such as 'The Fireman' in *Apusskidu Songs for Children* chosen by Beatrice Harrop, Peggy Blakeley and David Gadsby (A & C Black). (C4)

ACTIVITY: Collecting a football kit

Learning opportunity: Sorting clothes into sets, matching colours and counting the numbers in each set.

Early Learning Goal: Mathematical Development. Children will be able to count reliably up to ten everyday objects and use language such as 'more' or 'less' to compare two numbers.

Resources: Shirts, shorts and socks cut out from six different colours of card; a die with six faces of corresponding colours. The aim is to collect socks, shorts and a shirt in the same colour. At the end, encourage children to count how many sets they have and also how many they have of each type of clothing.

Key vocabulary: Names of the chosen colours, shorts, socks, shirt, numbers up to ten.

Organisation: Four children.

WHAT TO DO:

Show the group the clothes cut from card. Explain that they are clothes for a football player. Show the group the die and explain that they will take it in turns to throw the die and take a piece of clothing of the same colour. Play the game and when there are no more clothes to collect, ask the children to sort their clothes into colours. Does anyone have a matching set of shorts, shirt and socks? Who has the most socks? Who has the fewest shirts? Encourage children to count according to different criteria and to realise that different children will have more or fewer of the various items of clothing.

ACTIVITY: Jointed football player

Learning opportunity: Choosing colours and making patterns.

Early Learning Goal: Creative Development. Children will be able to explore colour, texture, shape, form and space in two dimensions.

Resources: A range of pictures depicting football players in a variety of team colours; for each child arms, legs and a body cut from card; brass fasteners; crayons in bright colours.

Key vocabulary: Names of chosen colours, football player, stripe, spot, dot, star.

Organisation: Small group.

WHAT TO DO:

Show children the cut-out body parts. Ask the group what they think they will make when they are joined together. Lay out one set to make a body. Show children the pictures of the football players. Explain that because all players in the same team wear the same uniform or strip it is easier to know who to pass the ball to. Look closely at the football clothes and encourage children to describe the patterns and colours. Invite the children to make a football strip for their person. What colour and pattern will the shirt have? What colour will the socks and shorts need to be if they are to match the shirt? When the body parts and clothes have been coloured, show children how to link the pieces together with brass fasteners.

DISPLAY

Cover a large noticeboard with green paper and stick on white lines to represent a football pitch. Invite children to position their jointed football players on the pitch. Help them to arrange the arms and legs to look like someone playing football. Cut out a football and cover it with black and white hexagons. Each day, change the place where the football is placed and encourage the children to spot where the ball has been kicked. Some days the ball may have been kicked so far that it is on another noticeboard, a window or even on the ceiling!

Week 5

CLOTHES FROM AROUND THE WORLD

PERSONAL, SOCIAL AND EMOTIONAL DEVELOPMENT

- Make a collection of dolls dressed in national costume. Invite children to bring in their own dolls to add to the display. Encourage them to describe what each one is wearing and to help in making labels for their countries of origin. (PS 2, 3, 8)

- Make a display of clothing from different countries. Help children to make small flags to represent the countries from which the clothes came. As a group, make a display of a world map with the clothes and flags. (PS1, 5, 8)

- Provide a range of clothes from different cultures for children to enjoy wearing in role-play situations. (PS10, 11)

COMMUNICATION, LANGUAGE AND LITERACY

- Together recite the nursery rhyme 'There was an old woman who lived in a shoe'. Provide clogs cut from card. Encourage children to decorate the shoe as a traditional Dutch clog, to draw pictures of the children who lived in the shoe and to write a name label. (L3, 17)

- Read *Katie Morag and the Wedding* by Mairi Hedderwick (Red Fox). Look closely at the pictures of the clothes people wore at the wedding. Who was wearing tartan? Show children some tartan materials and invite them to design a tartan for their own name. Make a book of the group's tartans with names written in by the children. (L17)

- Read *My Journey Around the World by Jeremy Bear* by Alison Morris (Oxford University Press). Talk to children about all the places which the teddy bear visited. What other places might the bear have liked to go to? What sorts of clothes would people wear in these places? Introduce a new

teddy bear to the group. Invite children to take it in turns to take the bear away at weekends and to record the bear's outing for a group book. (This activity can continue beyond the Clothes topic.) (L3)

MATHEMATICAL DEVELOPMENT

- Provide each child with a strip of corrugated card long enough to go around their head and a selection of coloured feathers to make a native American Indian head-dress with a repeating pattern (see activity opposite). (M8)

- Provide each child with a drawing of about ten identical feathers in a row. Ask them to colour the feathers in the same colour pattern as the head-dress they made. Display the pictures on a board and encourage children to match the patterns to their head-dresses. (M8)

- Show the children a piece of paisley material. (Paisley fabric is based upon an Indian mango design.) Provide each child with a cut-out mango shape. Encourage them to decorate the edge of the shape with large round sequins. Ask the children to count how many sequins they have used and help them to record the number in their shape. (M2, 3)

- Help children to sort a selection of national costume dolls according to different criteria, such as dolls wearing or not wearing aprons. Count the number of dolls in each set. (M2, 7)

KNOWLEDGE AND UNDERSTANDING OF THE WORLD

- Show children Japanese kimonos or pictures of kimonos. Encourage them to look at and describe the similarities and differences in colours and designs. (K2, 3)

- Invite a visitor to dress a child in a sari or kimono. Record the event by taking photographs. (K10)

- Provide a selection of travel brochures which contain pictures of people dressed in national costumes. Help the children to cut out their favourite costumes and to give reasons for their choices. Stick the pictures on the group's display of clothes from around the world. (K10)

PHYSICAL DEVELOPMENT

- Play the 'Around the world' game (see activity opposite). (PD1, 2, 3)

- Put out a circuit of coloured hoops ending with a mat representing home. Encourage the children to go on a journey, travelling in a variety of ways through the hoop countries. (PD2, 7)

- Repeat the journey activity but this time ask children to collect items such as bean bags or sponge balls as they travel through the countries and return home. (PD2, 6, 7)

CREATIVE DEVELOPMENT

- Play a selection of music from different countries including pan pipes from South America and Russian dance music. Encourage the children to enjoy moving in time with the music and clapping the rhythms. (C4)

- Provide each child with a large child-size kimono cut from white paper for decorating with bright, painted patterns. (C1)

- Invite children to make homes for the national costume dolls. Encourage them to think about the size of box they will need and to consider the decoration they think the doll would like for the inside of the home. When finished, use the homes for imaginative role play. (C1, 4)

ACTIVITY: Making a native American head-dress

Learning opportunity: Making repeating patterns.

Early Learning Goal: Mathematical Development. Children will be able to talk about, recognise and recreate simple patterns.

Resources: Strips of corrugated card about 60 x 5 cm; coloured feathers; stapler; picture of a native American Indian head-dress.

Key vocabulary: Feather, repeating pattern, native American Indian head-dress.

Organisation: Small group.

WHAT TO DO:

Show the group the picture of the native American Indian head-dress. Look at the colours of the feathers and the way that they are arranged. Explain that the children are going to make their own head-dresses. Take a handful of feathers and start to arrange them in a repeating pattern by sticking the ends of the feathers into a strip of corrugated card. As you place them, say aloud the colour of the feathers. After about five have been arranged, ask if anyone knows which colour feather is needed for the pattern to continue. Repeat the activity with a different pattern. Once all

children understand the need to make repeating patterns, help them to make their own head-dresses.

ACTIVITY: Travelling around the world

Learning opportunity: Listening and moving with imagination.

Early Learning Goal: Physical Development. Children will be able to move with confidence, imagination and in safety. They will move with control and co-ordination and show awareness of space, themselves and others.

Resources: A selection of national costume dolls familiar to the group; a globe.

Key vocabulary: Names of the countries corresponding to the chosen costume dolls, words to describe movement such as quietly, slowly, silently, on tip toe.

Organisation: Whole group in a large space.

WHAT TO DO:

Show the children the globe. Talk about what it is. Show the group where they live. Next show the costume dolls and ask children to name the countries from which they have come. Point to these places on the globe. Place the dolls around the room in positions where they are safe and can be seen clearly. Explain to the group that they are going to go on a journey around the world visiting all the countries that the dolls have come from. Use the dolls to represent the countries and tell a story of going around the world. Encourage children to listen carefully and to follow the descriptions for how to travel and what to do.

DISPLAY

Arrange the painted kimonos and the native American Indian head-dresses as if in a large shop window. Place the homes for national costume dolls on the floor nearby. In front of the homes, lay a long piece of dark material or black sugar paper with white lines down the centre for children to play on with toy cars. Use the mango designs to edge a large piece of material to represent the designs seen on some saris and drape this near the 'shop window'.

Week 6

FASHION SHOW

PERSONAL, SOCIAL AND EMOTIONAL DEVELOPMENT

- Introduce the fashion show which will take place at the end of the week and discuss all the jobs that will need to be done. (PS3, 4, 7)

- Read or tell the story of 'My Naughty Little Sister wins a Prize' in *My Naughty Little Sister* by Dorothy Edwards (Puffin). Talk about how the little sister probably felt when she was given the chance to wear a beautiful dress in a parade. Relate this to the group's fashion show and the kinds of clothes that children have and would like to wear. Also, discuss the kindness of the little sister when she gave away her prize. What would children in the group have done? (PS2, 3, 4)

COMMUNICATION, LANGUAGE AND LITERACY

- Make posters and invitations to advertise the forthcoming fashion show. (L16)

- Scribe for children the descriptions of the outfits they plan to model at the fashion show. (L2, 4)

- As a group, organise the order in which children will show their clothes. Talk about the way different sorts of clothes could be grouped together. Make a large programme for children to write in their names. Invite children to provide illustrations of their outfits. (L5, 7, 17)

MATHEMATICAL DEVELOPMENT

- Make bonnets from semi-circles (see activity opposite). (M9)

- Provide each child with a selection of paper triangle, squares, rectangles and circles. Ask them to use the shapes to make people dressed for a fashion parade. Which shapes would be good for hats? How could trousers be made? (M9)

- Turn the role-play area into an office for the fashion show. Include tickets with numbers, a phone and a cash register. Invite children to take turns in running the office and in being customers. Encourage the children to buy and sell tickets, to dial phone numbers given to them and to note and record the numbers of the sold tickets. (M1, 3, 11)

KNOWLEDGE AND UNDERSTANDING OF THE WORLD

- Make top hats from marshmallows and melted chocolate (see activity opposite). (K1, 3)

- Help children to take a photo of a friend wearing their parade hat, necklace and bracelet. Use the photos as part of a class fashion show book to record the event. (K7)

- Make a collection of family photographs taken at special occasions, such as weddings, to show people wearing hats. Set up a role-play shop with hats and plastic mirrors. Encourage children to be aware of the variety of the shapes of hats and the materials used to make them. (K2, 8)

PHYSICAL DEVELOPMENT

- Rehearse walking gracefully in a straight line, turning smoothly and standing still for the fashion show. (PD2)

- Enjoy having bean bag races in which children have to walk quickly with a bean bag balanced on their head. (PD2)

- Look at pictures of people wearing hooped skirts and practise poised walking with a hoop. Show children how to carry a hoop around their hips with straight arms, walk in a straight line, twirl and return. Help the children to imagine they are wearing long garments. (PD2)

CREATIVE DEVELOPMENT

- Sing 'My hat it has three corners' from *Okki-tokki-unga Action Songs for Children* chosen by Beatrice Harrop, Linda Friend and David Gadsby (A & C Black). Enjoy doing the actions. (C4)

- Use macaroni tubes coloured with food colouring or pieces cut from thick, brightly coloured plastic straws and string to make necklaces and bracelets for the fashion parade. (C1)

- Provide each child with a card hat template. Encourage children to decorate them using a variety of tactile textiles. (C1, 5)

ACTIVITY: Making bonnets

Learning opportunity: Describing shapes and making bonnets.

Early Learning Goal: Mathematical Development. Children will be able to use language such as 'circle' or 'bigger' to describe the shape and size of flat shapes.

Resources: For each child a semi-circle of coloured card with ribbon glued or stapled 5cm from the back edge (see diagram); a variety of brightly coloured regular shapes including sequins; glue; an example of

a made bonnet. (For longer lasting bonnets the card can be covered with felt.)

Key vocabulary: Bonnet, ribbon, names of shapes used, circle.

Organisation: Small group.

WHAT TO DO:

Show the group the made bonnet. Explain that everyone is going to make one and that those who wish to could wear them at the fashion show. Talk about the shape of the bonnet. What does it remind children of? Does anyone know its name? Demonstrate how two of the semi-circles can be joined to make a complete circle. As a group, look at the shapes which may be used to decorate the bonnets and invite children to select the ones they wish to use. Encourage children to name the shapes they choose and to compare the relative sizes of similar shapes. After the bonnets are made and have dried, encourage children to try them on and to look in mirrors.

your local area health and safety guidelines for cooking activities.

Key vocabulary: Marshmallow, top hat, melt, chocolate, hot, warm, cold.

Organisation: Small group.

WHAT TO DO:

Show the group the picture of the top hat and explain that they are going to use marshmallows and chocolate to make top hats to eat at the fashion show. Break up the cooking chocolate and place it in a bowl. Place this bowl in a bowl of warm water. Encourage children to watch the chocolate as it melts and to describe the changes. Talk about why the chocolate melts. When it has melted, invite children to take it in turns to spoon chocolate into each paper case and to place a marshmallow on top. Finally, help the children to place a small dab of chocolate on the top and a sweet. When it has set, talk about the way the chocolate is no longer melted and runny. Allow those children who are able to (check your records

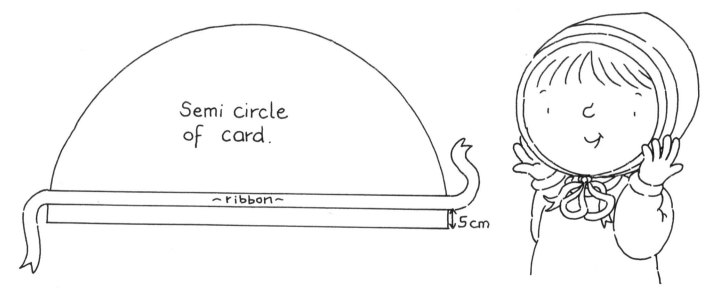

Semi circle of card.

~ribbon~

5cm

ACTIVITY: Making top hats

Learning opportunity: Observing and describing changes.

Early Learning Goal: Knowledge and Understanding of the World. Children will be able to investigate objects and materials using all of their senses as appropriate. They will look closely at change.

Resources: Sweet paper cases; pink and white marshmallows; small sweets for decoration; cooking utensils; warm water; a top hat or a picture of one;

first regarding children with food allergies) to eat a top hat and describe the tastes.

DISPLAY

Encourage children to help in the making of a display to advertise the forthcoming fashion show. Discuss the best place for the display. Put up the posters. Ask children to choose whether they will wear their native American Indian head-dress or their bonnet for the show and use the ones not being worn in the display. On a table, place the class book of photos taken by the children.

BRINGING IT ALL TOGETHER

THE FASHION SHOW

Talk to the children about the fashion show and its purpose. You might decide to use this as a fund-raising opportunity for a charity, a developing country, a current appeal or your own group. You may prefer simply to prepare and enjoy the event with children's families.

At the start of the topic, inform parents of the forthcoming fashion show. Explain that children will be making hats and jewellery. Ask parents to allow their children to pick a favourite outfit to wear on the day.

PREPARATIONS

During the topic children will each have made a hat and a necklace. They will have been involved in the production of descriptions of the clothes they plan to model.

Help the children to practise walking along a strip of carpet slowly whilst their description is being read and to think about how they can best show their audience what they are wearing. In addition, encourage children to think about how they can help their friends by being a good audience, too. Invite some children to be responsible with an adult for welcoming parents and ask others to show the guests to their seats.

ON THE DAY

Invite a parent to record the show with a video camera and another to take photographs for making a big group book.

Seat children close to a strip of carpet laid out as a catwalk where they can easily get into position for their turn but can also see their friends. Encourage children to clap their friends after each turn.

At the end of the event, involve children in handing out marshmallow top hats and a cold drink and in acting as tour guides of all the displays which have happened during the Clothes topic.

If the event is to raise money also involve the children in collecting and counting the money.

RESOURCES

RESOURCES TO COLLECT

- National costume dolls.
- Dressing-up clothes from a variety of countries.
- Old socks, tights, boots and shoes.
- Feathers.
- Sequins.

EVERYDAY RESOURCES

- Boxes, large and small for modelling
- Papers and cards of different weights, colours and textures, for example sugar, corrugated card, silver and shiny papers.
- Dry powder paints for mixing and mixed paints for covering large areas and printing activities
- Different sized paint brushes from household brushes to thin brushes for delicate work and a variety of paint mixing containers.
- A variety of drawing and colouring pencils, crayons, pastels, charcoals, and so on.
- Additional decorative and finishing materials such as sequins, foils, glitter, tinsel, shiny wool and threads, beads, pieces of textiles, parcel ribbon.
- Table covers.
- Pasta.

STORIES

Mrs Lather's Laundry by Allan Ahlberg (Puffin).

My Naughty Little Sister by Dorothy Edwards (Puffin).

My Journey Around the World by Jeremy Bear, text by Alison Morris (Oxford University Press).

Paddington's Story Book Treasury by Michael Bond (Harper Collins).

Mrs Jollipop by Dick King-Smith (Macdonald Young Books).

Jerry's Trousers by Nigel Boswall and David Melling (Macmillan).

Katie Morag and the Wedding by Mairi Hedderwick (Red Fox).

Tattybogle by Sandra Horn and Ken Brown (Hodder Children's Books).

SONGS

Okki-tokki-unga Action Songs for Children chosen by Beatrice Harrop, Linda Friend and David Gadsby (A & C Black).

Apusskido Songs for children chosen by Beatrice Harrop, Peggy Blakely and David Gadsby (A & C Black).

POEMS

This Little Puffin by Elizabeth Matterson (Puffin).

Out and About by Shirley Hughes (Walker Books).

Pudding and Pie chosen by Sarah Williams (Oxford University Press).

ICT

'Dress the Teddy' on *My World* by North West SEMERC, Oldham (Tel. 0161 627 4469).

All books were available from leading booksellers at the time of writing.

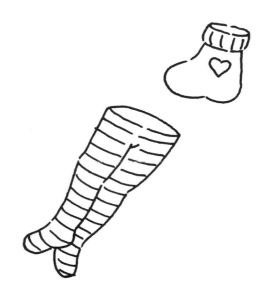

COLLECTING EVIDENCE OF CHILDREN'S LEARNING

Monitoring children's development is an important task. Keeping a record of children's achievements will help you to see progress and will draw attention to those who are having difficulties for some reason. If a child needs additional professional help, such as speech therapy, your records will provide valuable evidence.

Records should be the result of collaboration between group leaders, parents and carers. Parents should be made aware of your record keeping policies when their child joins your group. Show them the type of records you are keeping and make sure they understand that they have an opportunity to contribute. As a general rule, your records should form an open document. Any parent should have access to records relating to his or her child. Take regular opportunities to talk to parents about children's progress. If you have formal discussions regarding children about whom you have particular concerns, a dated record of the main points should be kept.

KEEPING IT MANAGEABLE

Records should be helpful in informing group leaders, adult helpers and parents and always be for the benefit of the child. However, keeping records of every aspect of each child's development can become a difficult task. The sample shown will help to keep records manageable and useful. The golden rule is to keep them simple.

Observations will basically fall into three categories:

- **Spontaneous records:** Sometimes you will want to make a note of observations as they happen, for example when a child is heard counting cars accurately during a play activity, or is seen to play collaboratively for the first time.

- **Planned observations:** Sometimes you will plan to make observations of children's developing skills in their everyday activities. Using the learning opportunity identified for an activity will help you to make appropriate judgements about children's capabilities and to record them systematically.

To collect information:

- talk to children about their activities and listen to their responses;

- listen to children talking to each other;

- observe children's work such as early writing, drawings, paintings and 3-d models. (Keeping photocopies or photographs is sometimes useful.)

Sometimes you may wish to set up 'one-off' activities for the purposes of monitoring development. Some groups, for example, ask children to make a drawing of themselves at the beginning of each term to record their progressing skills in both co-ordination and observation. Do not attempt to make records following every activity!

- **Reflective observations:** It is useful to spend regular time reflecting on the progress of a few children (about four children each week). Aim to make some brief comments about each child every half term.

INFORMING YOUR PLANNING

Collecting evidence about children's progress is time-consuming but it essential. When you are planning, use the information you have collected to help you to decide what learning opportunities you need to provide next for children. For example, a child who has poor pencil or brush control will benefit from more play with dough or construction toys to build the strength of hand muscles.

Example of recording chart

Name: Lucy Field		D.O.B. 18.2.97		Date of entry: 13.9.00	
Term	**Personal, Social and Emotional**	**Communication, Language and Literacy**	**Mathematical Development**	**Knowledge and Understanding**	**Physical Development**	**Creative Development**
ONE	Reluctant to say goodbye to mother. Prefers adult company. 20.9.00 EMH	Enjoys listening to stories. 'Jerry's Trousers' is a particular favourite. Can write first name. Good pencil grip. 20.10.00 EMH	Is able to say numbers to ten and count accurately five objects. Recognises and names triangle, square and circle 5/11/00 EHL	Eager to ask questions. Was fascinated by the shoe grip experiment. 16.10.00 LSS	Can balance on one leg. Loves climbing on the big apparatus Good at aiming bean bags. 16.10.00 AC	Enjoys painting particularly when mixing own colours. 16.10.99 EHL
TWO						
THREE						

SKILLS OVERVIEW OF SIX-WEEK PLAN

Week	Topic focus	Personal, Social and Emotional Development	Communication, Language and Literacy	Mathematical Development	Knowledge and Understanding of the World	Physical Development	Creative Development
1	My clothes	Listening; Expressing emotions; Taking turns; Dressing independently	Listening Writing Recognising initial sounds	Recognising 2-d shapes Counting; Making repeating patterns	Making observations Comparing Describing	Moving with control and imagination	Collage Painting
2	Socks and shoes	Listening Developing independence	Rhyming; Listening Talking; Writing	Counting Measuring	Making observations Comparing; Describing	Moving with control and coordination	Role play Using materials Making sounds
3	Clothes for all weathers	Speaking; Listening Dressing independently Taking turns	Listening to stories Writing	Recognising patterns Counting Recognising numbers	Comparing similarities and differences Observing	Moving with confidence, imagination and safety	Making sun hats Responding to what they touch and feel
4	Uniforms	Taking turns; Listening Forming good relationships	Talking; Listening to stories Writing	Sorting Recognising 2-d shapes Counting	Talking Observing Investigating	Moving with control, coordination and awareness of space	Role play; Singing Making jointed people
5	Clothes from around the world	Talking; Respecting cultures; Using resources independently	Writing Listening to stories Discussing	Counting; Sorting Making repeating patterns	Observing Knowing about cultures	Moving with control Travelling through equipment	Dancing Making models Painting
6	Fashion show	Expressing emotions Collaborative planning	Writing for a purpose Talking	Recognising 2-d shapes Recognising numbers Using mathematical ideas	Observing Describing; Investigating Comparing	Moving with control and coordination	Singing Collage Threading

HOME LINKS

The theme of Clothes lends itself to useful links with children's homes and families. Through working together, children and adults gain respect for each other and build comfortable and confident relationships.

ESTABLISHING PARTNERSHIPS

- Keep parents informed about the topic of Clothes and the themes for each week. By understanding the work of the group, parents will enjoy the involvement of contributing ideas, time and resources.

- Photocopy the parent's page for each child to take home.

- Invite friends, childminders and families to share all or part of the fashion show.

VISITING ENTHUSIASTS

- Invite known adults to come to the group to talk about uniforms and children to talk about uniforms worn by Brownies, Scouts, and so on.

- Invite someone who wears a sari to demonstrate how one is put on.

RESOURCE REQUESTS

- Ask parents to contribute old shoes and boots for sorting, printing and science activities.

- Feathers, scraps of wool and fabric, sequins and ribbons are invaluable for collage work and a wide range of interesting activities related to clothes.

- National costume dolls, baby clothes once worn by the children and hats will all be useful. Ensure that items lent can be safely handled by the children.

THE FASHION SHOW

- It is always useful to have extra adults at times such as the fashion show for helping children to dress and to be in the right place at the right time!

- Refreshments for after the show will always be appreciated and many parents will enjoy making biscuits and buns in the shapes of hats, shoes and other items of clothing.